ANIMALS
ANIMALS

GORILLAS

BY JUDITH JANGO-COHEN

BENCHMARK BOOKS

MARSHALL CAVENDISH
NEW YORK

Dedicated to my parents, Bob and Grace Jango, who taught me the meaning of family.

j. j. c.

Series Consultant

James Doherty

General Curator

Bronx Zoo, New York

Benchmark Books

Marshall Cavendish Corporation

99 White Plains Road

Tarrytown, NY 10591-9001

www.marshallcavendish.com

Text copyright © 2003 by Judith Jango-Cohen

Library of Congress Cataloging-in-Publication Data

Jango-Cohen, Judith.

Gorillas / by Judith Jango-Cohen.

p. cm. – (Animals, animals)

Includes bibliographical references and index

Summary: Describes the physical characteristics, behavior, and habitat of the largest of the great apes.

ISBN 0-7614-1444-4

1. Gorilla–Juvenile literature. [1. Gorilla.] I. Title. II. Series.

QL737.P96 J265 2002

599.884–dc21

2001006993

Photo Research by Anne Burns Images

Cover photo: Animals/Animals:Jim Tuten

Photographs in this book are used by permission and through the courtesy of: *Peter Arnold, Inc.*: Michael Gunther-Bios, 4, 38; Martin Harvey, 15; Klaus Paysan, 16; Evelyn Gallardo, 33; Y.Arthus-Bertrand, 34, 40. *Visuals Unlimited*: Joe McDonald, 6; Gary W. Carter, 22. *Animals/Animals*: Robert P. Comport, 8; Ralph Reinhold, 9; Jim Tutten 14 (left); A.Plumtre, 18; Roger Aitkenhead, 19; S.Turner, 20; Gerard Lacz, 26; Bruce Davidson, 28; Murray G.Bertram, Jr., 30; Joe McDonald, 32; Patti Murray, 42. Jason Laure:10, 14 (left). Eliot Cohen: 14 (right). *The Gorilla Foundation*: 13. *Photo Researchers, Inc*: Bildarchiv Okapia, 36–37.

Printed in Hong Kong

1 3 5 6 4 2

C O N T E N T S

1
INTRODUCING GORILLAS

In an open patch of forest, a gorilla family rests. The older ones stretch out in the warm sunshine and slip off to sleep. Two young gorillas that are too fidgety to nap chase each other through the trees. There in the woods, almost hidden in the thick bushes, the two gorillas find a baby antelope. One gorilla lifts the fawn's head and sniffs its face. The other gorilla pulls on its legs. For almost an hour the little gorillas poke at the baby and stroke its fur. Finally, their curiosity satisfied, they wander back to their family.

Gorillas are curious animals. This is a sign of intelligence, one of the qualities of the great ape family. Gorillas are the largest members of this family, which also includes orangutans, chimpanzees, and bonobos. Scientists can tell that apes are intelligent by looking at their skulls. The skull is large compared to the size of the animal. In fact, a baby gorilla's brain is about the same size as a human baby's. But as people grow their brains become larger than the gorilla's.

A MOTHER GORILLA'S ARMS FORM A FURRY CRADLE FOR HER BABY.

CHIMPANZEES AND GORILLAS ARE APES SO, UNLIKE MONKEYS, THEY DO NOT HAVE TAILS.

6

In addition to a large braincase, a gorilla's skull also has two eye sockets that face forward. This gives gorillas binocular vision, which means that both eyes can focus together on the same object. With binocular vision gorillas can correctly judge the distance of an object, such as a nearby tree branch.

Binocular vision aids gorillas when they are hanging around in trees. But it is their hands and feet that help get them up there. In the 1800s scientists *classified* gorillas as "quadrumana," meaning four–handed. This is because their big toe grips like a thumb. So while gorillas climb, they can clasp onto branches with both their hands and their feet.

Up in the trees gorillas' feet work like human hands, grabbing and grasping. Down on the ground their hands work like our feet do. Gorillas walk by swinging their long arms ahead of their body with closed hands. They pull themselves forward on the knuckles of their closed hands. Thick skin cushions their five fingers, and tough nails protect their fingertips.

LIKE HUMANS, GORILLAS HAVE THREE-DIMENSIONAL COLOR VISION.

The only place to find curious, knuckle-walking, tree-climbing gorillas is in the forests of Africa. They live along the *equator* in the western and east–central part of the continent. Scientists once believed that all gorillas were similar enough to be classified as one *species*. But new evidence about gorilla body structure and behavior has led some scientists to separate gorillas into two species: the western gorilla and the eastern gorilla. Some researchers think that there are two *subspecies* of the western gorilla and three of the eastern gorilla.

DENSE RAIN FORESTS PROVIDE GORILLAS WITH A WEALTH OF FOOD.

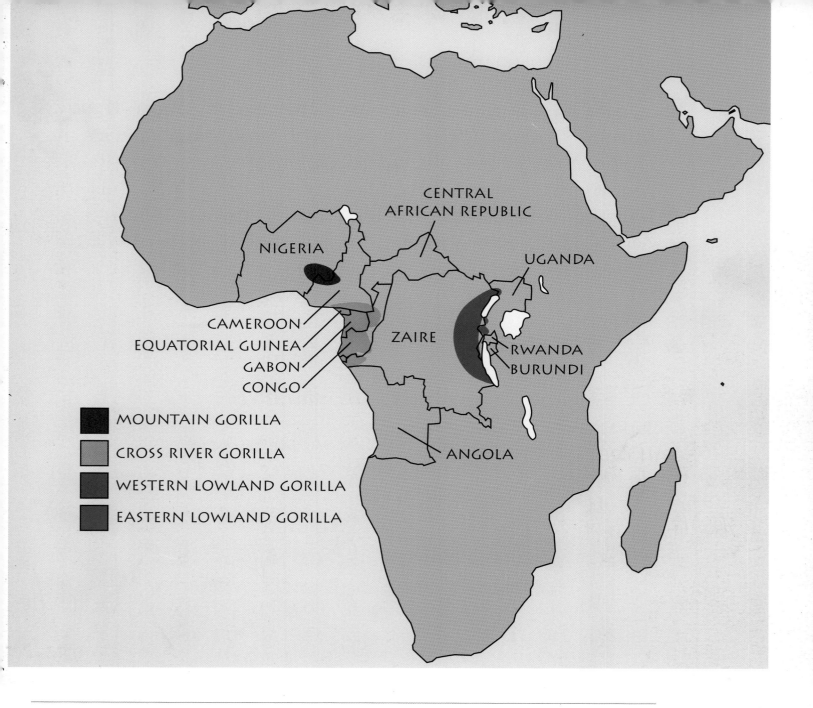

CENTRAL
AFRICAN REPUBLIC

NIGERIA

UGANDA

CAMEROON

EQUATORIAL GUINEA

ZAIRE

GABON

CONGO

RWANDA
BURUNDI

MOUNTAIN GORILLA

CROSS RIVER GORILLA

WESTERN LOWLAND GORILLA

EASTERN LOWLAND GORILLA

ANGOLA

THIS MAP SHOWS THE CURRENT RANGES, OR LIVING AREAS, OF THE TWO
GORILLA SPECIES.

The two gorilla species are separated by more than six hundred miles (966 km). So over time each species has changed as it has *adapted* to different environments. The mountain gorilla, a subspecies of eastern gorilla, has long hair that protects it in the cool, rainy Virunga Mountains of Africa. The western lowland gorilla has short fur because it lives in the humid rain forests of warmer altitudes.

HOW ARE SCIENTISTS AND GORILLAS ALIKE?

BOTH ARE CURIOUS. DR. FRANCINE PATTERSON IS A SCIENTIST WHO WANTED TO KNOW IF GORILLAS WERE INTELLIGENT ENOUGH TO LEARN LANGUAGE. IN 1972 SHE BEGAN TEACHING AMERICAN SIGN LANGUAGE (ASL) TO A GORILLA NAMED KOKO. TODAY KOKO HAS LEARNED OVER ONE THOUSAND SIGNS. BUT SOMETIMES SHE FORGETS A WORD. WHEN KOKO COULDN'T REMEMBER THE SIGN FOR HER PINOCCHIO DOLL, SHE MADE UP HER OWN WORD. SHE CALLED IT "ELEPHANT BABY."

Eastern or western, lowland or mountain, all gorillas share similar lives. They sleep, feed, and play in the forest with their family gathered around them.

DR. FRANCINE PATTERSON INTRODUCES KOKO TO A KITTEN.

A WESTERN
LOWLAND GORILLA

FEMALES LIKE THIS ONE
WEIGH FROM 150 TO 200
LBS (68-91 KG), ABOUT HALF
AS MUCH AS A MALE.

THIS MOUNTAIN GORILLA
HAS THE HIGH HEAD CREST
AND BARE CHEST FOUND
ONLY IN ADULT MALES.

THE WESTERN GORILLA IS THE
SPECIES MOST COMMONLY
SEEN IN ZOOS.

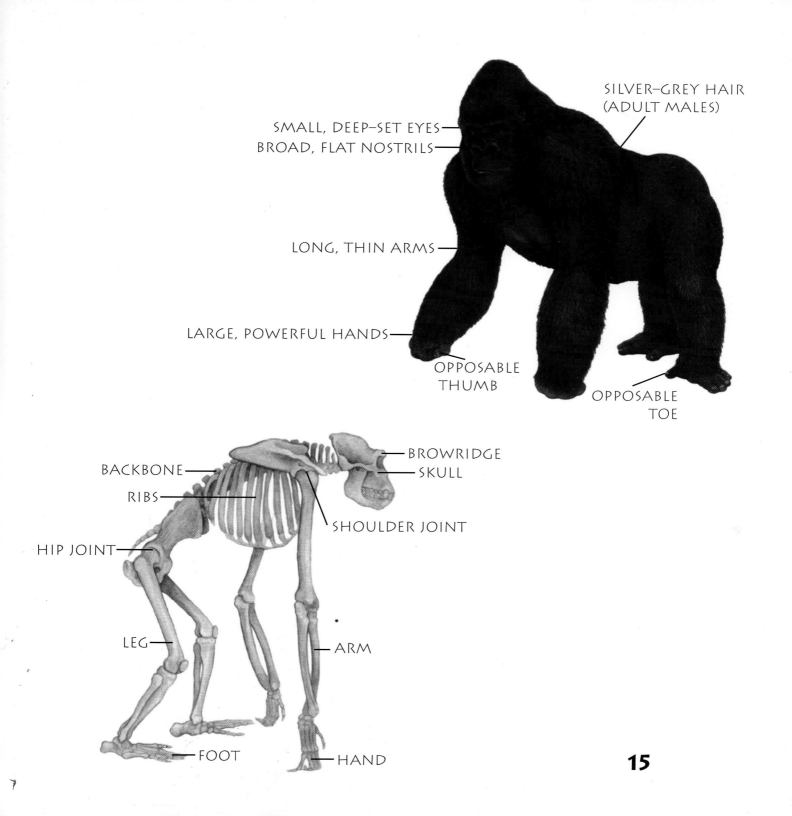

SILVER–GREY HAIR
(ADULT MALES)

SMALL, DEEP–SET EYES

BROAD, FLAT NOSTRILS

LONG, THIN ARMS

LARGE, POWERFUL HANDS

OPPOSABLE
THUMB

OPPOSABLE
TOE

BROWRIDGE

BACKBONE

SKULL

RIBS

SHOULDER JOINT

HIP JOINT

LEG

ARM

FOOT

HAND

15

2
FOREST FAMILY

A female mountain gorilla sits against a tree, arms hugging her chest. Above one furry forearm the top of a tiny black head is barely visible. The female is holding a four-pound (1.81 kg) newborn.

The baby's sibling peeks over the mother's arm at the toothless, squinty-eyed infant. Its tiny hand opens, revealing a pink palm. An older sibling reaches out toward the infant, but the mother raises an arm in protection.

The baby squirms and stretches its head, as if it is looking for something. Finding the mother's nipple, a meal of warm milk fills its stomach, and the baby falls asleep. A mother gorilla may nurse its young for three years.

This family, or troop, also includes an eight-month-old gorilla that began crawling at four months. Its favorite way to travel, though, is on its mother's back.

YOUNG GORILLAS LIKE TO WRESTLE, PLAY CATCH, AND ROMP THROUGH THE TREES.

DESPITE THEIR GREAT SIZE, ADULT SILVERBACKS ARE EXTREMELY GENTLE WHEN HANDLING INFANTS.

Two more little ones, a two– and three–year–old, chase each other around their drowsy father. They scramble over the mounds of his huge body. Then they climb up his silvered back and slide down. As they run up for another ride, the *silverback* gets up. He grunts at the two youngsters halfheartedly and then strolls off.

19

WHILE OLDER GORILLAS REST AND EAT, YOUNGSTERS OFTEN PLAY.

The rest of the troop notices that the silverback is up. He has decided that it is time to search for a morning feeding spot. The whole family follows along, except for one little gorilla swinging from the top of a bamboo tree. The silverback swats the trunk with his big hand. The tree cracks and sways, and the young gorilla jumps down to join its family.

THE AVERAGE GORILLA TROOP IS BIGGER THAN MOST HUMAN FAMILIES. IT OFTEN INCLUDES SEVERAL YOUNG, FROM NEWBORN TO AGE EIGHT, AND A FEW ADULT FEMALES. THERE MAY ALSO BE YOUNG MALES, CALLED BLACKBACKS, WHO WILL STAY IN THE TROOP UNTIL SOME TIME DURING THEIR TENTH TO THIRTEENTH YEAR. WHEN THEY REACH ADULTHOOD AND THE FUR ON THEIR BACKS TURNS SILVER, THEY USUALLY LEAVE THE TROOP TO FORM A FAMILY OF THEIR OWN. SOME GROUPS MAY HAVE SEVERAL OLDER MALES, BUT ONLY ONE IS THE BOSS.

3
SNACKING AND NAPPING

As gorillas travel through the forest, they leave a trace behind. Rows of flattened plants mark their route. Pressed into scattered mud patches are the patterns of their knuckle prints. The gorillas also leave warm dung. Their dung looks much like horse manure because most of their diet is made of plants.

The family's trail stops in front of a cavelike hollow below a ridge of trees. The silverback enters the hollow alone, disappearing through a tangle of tree roots. Inside, he digs into the bank, crumbles up handfuls of soil, and shovels them into his mouth. Like a vitamin pill, this soil contains calcium, iron, and salt.

Finally, the silverback plods out of the cave, looking like a dusty old bear. Now the others, who have been waiting impatiently, take their turns. The older gorillas enter first,

GORILLAS SELDOM DRINK WATER, AS THEY RECEIVE SO MUCH MOISTURE FROM THE PLANTS THEY EAT.

followed by the youngsters. Cramped inside, the gorillas begin to quarrel. Grunts and shrieks can be heard coming from the cave.

When the last straggler leaves the dugout hollow, the gorillas move on. Up ahead, in a sunny clearing, the sil–verback plops down. Each gorilla claims a spot, as if at a picnic. A blackback reaches out leisurely with its long arm and rips a limb from a tree. Holding it like an ear of corn, he nibbles on its mossy coating. A female pulls a chunk of bark from a trunk and laps up some plump grubs.

DO YOU EVER EAT FOOD THAT STINGS YOU? GORILLAS SOMETIMES DO. YOUNG GORILLAS EAGERLY DIG UP CLODS OF SOIL THAT ARE QUIVERING WITH ANTS. THEN THEY GOBBLE UP THE BUGS. THE FEAST USUALLY ENDS WHEN SOME OF THE MEAL ESCAPES AND STARTS TO BITE. GORILLAS ALSO ENJOY A STINGING PLANT CALLED NETTLE. TO AVOID THE EDGES OF THE LEAVES, WHICH STING, THEY FOLD THE LEAVES OVER. THEN THEY POP THE LEAVES INTO THEIR MOUTHS.

EVERY MORNING GORILLAS SET OFF IN SEARCH OF THEIR FAVORITE FOODS.

FOR THIS YOUNG GORILLA, A TREE IS THE PERFECT PLACE TO PLAY AND FEED.

Another female sits nearby with an infant in her lap. While the mother munches on crisp wild celery sticks, the three-month-old reaches out for her own stalk. Her aim is not good yet, but after a few tries she finally grabs one. Although she cannot peel it properly, gnawing on it makes her gums feel better while she is teething. Sometimes she stops chewing to pick up fallen bits of celery that her mother has dropped.

Meanwhile, two young gorillas scramble up a tree toward an unexpected treat. Sticking out from the trunk, like a shelf, is a stiff fungus. The gorillas try to pry it off with their fingers, but it doesn't budge. So instead, they wrap their legs around the tree and nibble the fungus from there.

GORILLAS HELP TREES TO GROW. WHEN THEY EAT FRUIT, THE SEEDS ARE SCATTERED THROUGHOUT THE FOREST IN THEIR DUNG.

AFTER THEIR MIDMORNING MEAL, GORILLAS REST AND GROOM ONE ANOTHER.

Once they've finished their snack, they wrestle on a thick limb. This sends a rain of leaves and loose bark onto the adults lounging below. Then, the two curl up in a mossy crook of the tree and drift off to sleep.

Most of the adults are finishing their morning meal. Purring like contented cats, they lie down in the sun. A mother sleepily watches a six–month–old wriggle and crawl over her stomach. Picking up the baby, she playfully dangles him overhead. Then she holds the infant in her lap and begins to groom him. Parting the baby's fur, the mother picks out dirt, dead skin, and insects. After a few minutes, she plops the squirming baby back onto her stomach.

Soon the family is asleep, except for one young gorilla. With no one to play with, she is amusing herself by catching flies. Like a curious science student, she plucks her specimens apart and examines every piece.

4
SILVERBACK LEADER

After their midmorning meal and a long nap, the troop is ready to move. They wander along an open ridge, nib-bling on leaves and juicy stalks. Suddenly, on an opposite ridge, a young silverback emerges from the bushes. Keeping an eye on the family, he begins to strut back and forth. From time to time he unleashes a series of hoots. Then, standing up straight, the young silverback pounds its cupped palms against its chest. This chest beating is followed by the crack and snap of branches breaking.

The gorilla family has seen this lone silverback before trying to lure young females away from their troop. They don't pay much attention, though, until the *display* stops and the stranger begins to climb toward their ridge. The troop's silverback marches down to meet him, while the others watch silently. Then the lone gorilla stands up, beats his chest again, and smashes down more branches.

EVER ALERT, SILVERBACKS WATCH OVER THE SAFETY OF THE TROOP.

The older silverback answers with a majestic roar. Then he charges the younger male, who retreats down the ridge. The older silverback does not follow, but stares after his fleeing rival. Finally he turns and mounts the hill to rejoin his family.

FEMALES AND YOUNGSTERS SOMETIMES NEST IN TREES, UNLIKE THE HEAVIER SILVERBACKS.

After this encounter, the silverback slows the group's pace, allowing them frequent stops to rest and feed. Calmly he guides them toward the area where they will sleep for the night. But changing his mind, the silverback turns and leads them off in a new direction. Ahead, along their former path, is a danger he knows well. A dozen arched bamboo poles rise from a fence of ferns. Attached to each springy pole are wire nooses hidden in the dirt–*poachers'* traps!

33

A YOUNG GORILLA USUALLY SLEEPS IN ITS MOTHER'S NEST UNTIL IT IS THREE
OR FOUR YEARS OLD AND A NEW BABY ARRIVES.

These traps are not meant for the gorillas. They are set to catch antelope. But they can sometimes snare a gorilla's hand or foot. Gorillas are usually strong enough to break free of the bamboo pole. But the wire noose may retain its tight grip. Sometimes a silverback can save a family member by pulling the noose off with his teeth. Otherwise the wire digs into the skin until the gorilla dies from an infection.

Fortunately, the gorilla troop has avoided the traps and settles down for the evening. The silverback begins building his night nest at the base of the hill. He skillfully bends back a circle of stalks and tucks the leafy tops beneath him.

Farther up the hill, the rest of the family follows his example. A two-year-old gorilla, in its first attempt at building a nest, folds back a cluster of stems. When he perches on top of them, the plants pop back up. Next he tries lying down on them. But the bouncy stalks will not stay put. Finally, swatting at the springy stems, he runs off to snuggle in his mother's nest.

Some of the females and young gorillas are making beds in the forks of trees. They push down long limbs and then weave in smaller branches. As they lounge in their nests, the setting sun glitters through a veil of rain. With arms folded over their chests, the family huddles together in the mist.

IMAGINE A FOUR-HUNDRED-POUND (181 KG) WESTERN GORILLA JUMPING INTO A SWAMPY POOL AND SLAPPING THE WATER WITH HIS POWERFUL PALMS. SCIENTISTS THINK GORILLAS DO THIS TO AVOID A FIGHT. BY DISPLAYING THEIR STRENGTH, THE GORILLAS PROBABLY HOPE TO DISCOURAGE RIVAL SILVERBACKS FROM COMPETING FOR FEMALES.

A CALL OF ALARM FROM A SILVERBACK MOUNTAIN GORILLA WARNS THE TROOP OF DANGER.

5
GORILLAS AND PEOPLE

In an open patch of old forest, a gorilla family rests. Suddenly, something moves toward them in the forest. Out of the woods walks a guide and six tourists. They have come to Virunga National Park in Africa to see the mountain gorillas. The gorilla family knows this guide. For two years he has followed them through the forest until they have become *habituated* to him. Now they no longer run away.

The guide motions for his group to crouch down. Standing up might make the gorillas nervous. Keeping his eyes on the silverback, the guide imitates a gorilla's feeding sounds to put the troop at ease. The tourists watch as an infant crawls toward them. But they must not touch her. Their guide has explained that gorillas can die from human diseases such as pneumonia, measles, and tuberculosis.

Allowing tourists near the gorillas like this can invite problems, but it can also benefit the gorillas. The money

GORILLAS WHO HAVE BECOME HABITUATED TO PEOPLE MAY BECOME LESS AFRAID OF HUNTERS.

Dian Fossey was a scientist who traveled to the Virunga Mountains in 1967 to study the gorillas. When Dian first arrived, the gorillas were not habituated to her. So when–ever she approached, they would run off and hide. One day, to get a better view of them, Dian began to climb a tree. Grunting and grumbling, she made her way up the slippery trunk. But when she looked down from her perch, she discovered that the whole gorilla family had come out of hiding to watch her clumsy climbing. All they needed to complete their entertainment, Dian later wrote, were some "gorilla–sized bags of popcorn."

tourists bring to the park helps to pay for their protection. Also, with people around, poachers are less likely to enter the area. Although hunting is illegal in the parks, rangers have trouble patrolling the entire forest.

People are not supposed to hunt gorillas because they are *endangered*. But most gorillas do not live in protected parks. So poachers sometimes kill gorillas and sell them for their meat. Another threat to gorillas living outside parks is the loss of their *habitat*. As the population of Africa swells, forests are cut down for farms, cattle ranching, and lumber. Gorillas are then squeezed into shrinking pockets of forest. As a result, some people fear that gorillas might become *extinct*.

Organizations such as the International Gorilla Conservation Program and the Dian Fossey Gorilla Fund are working hard to prevent this. These *conservation groups* raise money to protect gorillas from poachers and to preserve their habitat. They also educate local people about this endangered species. Many Africans now work in parks as guides and rangers. Conservation groups also support tourist programs. But they make sure that the groups are small and do not visit the gorillas for too long.

After about an hour of watching the gorillas, the guide tells the six members of his group that it is time to go. Walking slowly away, the visitors turn back for one last look. Soon the silverback gets up, ending the midday rest period. As he leads his family on, the gorillas fade into the foliage, like shadows.

TO SAVE GORILLAS, WE MUST PRESERVE THEIR RAIN FOREST HOME.

adapt: to change in ways that help living things to survive better

American Sign Language: language for the hearing impaired that uses hand motions to form words

classify: to organize living things into groups based on similar traits

conservation groups: organizations that work to protect living things and their habitats

display: sounds and behaviors used by a silverback when he is threatened

endangered: threatened with becoming extinct

equator: an imaginary line around the earth that represents the halfway point between the North and South Poles

extinct: no longer existing

habitat: the place where a plant or animal lives

habituated: familiar with and unafraid of

poacher: a person who hunts animals where it is not allowed

silverback: an adult male gorilla whose back fur has begun to turn silver

species: a single type of living thing

subspecies: a population of animals within a species

BOOKS

Bailey, Jill. *Gorilla Rescue*. Austin, TX: Raintree Steck–Vaughn, 1990.

Bright, Michael. *Mountain Gorilla*. New York: Gloucester Press, 1989.

Burgel, Paul Hermann, and Manfred Hartwig. *Gorillas*. Minneapolis, MN: Carolrhoda Books, Inc., 1992.

Fossey, Dian. *Gorillas in the Mist*. New York: Hougton Mifflin, 2000.

Lewin, Ted and Betsy. *Gorilla Walk*. New York: Lothrop, Lee & Shepard Books, 1999.

McNulty, Faith. *With Love from Koko*. New York: Scholastic Inc., 1990.

Miller–Schroeder, Patricia. *Gorillas*. Austin, TX: Raintree Steck–Vaughn, 1997.

Patterson, Dr. Francine. *Koko-Love: Conversations with a Signing Gorilla*. New York: Dutton Children's Books, 1999.

Redmond, Ian. *Gorillas*. New York: The Bookwright Press, 1991.

–––.*Gorilla, Monkey & Ape*. New York: Dorling Kindersley, 2000.

Schott, Jane. *Dian Fossey and the Mountain Gorillas*. Minneapolis, MN: Carolrhoda Books, 2000.

Simon, Seymour. *Gorillas*. New York: HarperCollins Publishers, 2000.

VIDEOS

Gorilla. National Geographic Society, 1981.

Gorillas. Kodak/Sierra Club Series, 1988.

Gorillas. Time–Life, 1989.

Twilight of the Gorilla. Mutual of Omaha, 1988.

WEBSITES

The Dian Fossey Gorilla Fund International

http://www.gorillafund.org

http://www.dianfossey.org

The Gorilla Foundation

http://www.gorilla.org or http://www.koko.org

African Wildlife Foundation: Mountain Gorilla

http://www.awf.org/wildlives/149

ABOUT THE AUTHOR

Judith Jango–Cohen had a great time observing gorillas at the Franklin Park Zoo in Boston and at Washington D.C.'s National Zoological Park. Besides *Gorillas*, Judith has written, and sometimes photographed, eighteen other books for children. You can learn more about her work at www.agpix.com/cohen.

INDEX

Page numbers for illustrations are in **boldface.**